The Recently Deflowered Girl

Hyacinthe Phypps

The Recently Deflowered Girl

The Right Thing To Say
On Every Dubious
Occasion

HYACINTHE PHYPPS

Drawings by Edward Gorey

BLOOMSBURY

London   Berlin   New York

This edition published by Bloomsbury in Great Britain 2010
First published in the United States by Chelsea House in 1965

All papers used by Bloomsbury are natural, recyclable
products made from wood grown in well-managed forests.
The manufacturing processes conform to the environmental
regulations of the country of origin.

Bloomsbury Publishing Plc, 36 Soho Square, London W1D 3QY

A CIP catalogue record for this book
is available from the British Library

ISBN 978 1 4088 0517 6

1 3 5 7 9 10 8 6 4 2

Printed and bound in China
by Hung Hing Offset Printing Company Ltd

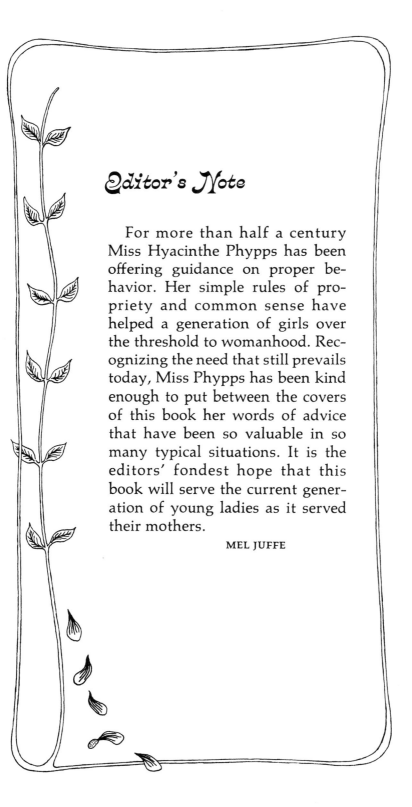

Editor's Note

For more than half a century Miss Hyacinthe Phypps has been offering guidance on proper behavior. Her simple rules of propriety and common sense have helped a generation of girls over the threshold to womanhood. Recognizing the need that still prevails today, Miss Phypps has been kind enough to put between the covers of this book her words of advice that have been so valuable in so many typical situations. It is the editors' fondest hope that this book will serve the current generation of young ladies as it served their mothers.

MEL JUFFE

Deflowerment on Blind Date

You accept blind date on phone with glib young man. He proves still more charming in person and takes flower.

On saying goodnight, you remark, "Incidentally, I don't think you ever did mention your last name, Joe."

He gives this some thought, then chuckles and says, "Maybe it's better that way."

You say (slyly): "Goodnight, Mr. Johnson."

Since more persons in America have the last name Johnson than any other, you are, at least, most likely to be correct with the name Johnson in this situation.

MISS H. P.

9

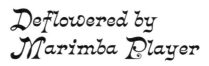

Deflowered by Marimba Player

After being deflowered, you discover that your parents refuse to give consent to marriage with mustachioed marimba player.

You are prevented from arranging another rendezvous, but you see him by chance at Junior League charity tea dance. He is playing in rhumba band. At intermission, you meet.

You say, "I'm terribly sorry, Harold, but my parents won't let me marry you."

He says, "That's all right, baby. I've been happily married for years."

You say: "How did your wife get *her* parents' consent?"

Your main difficulty apparently is in getting the consent of your parents. It is wise to learn how other girls get theirs. MISS H. P.

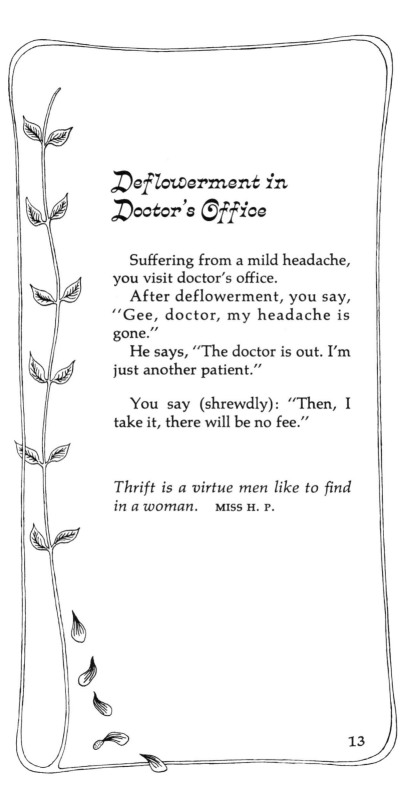

Deflowerment in Doctor's Office

Suffering from a mild headache, you visit doctor's office.

After deflowerment, you say, "Gee, doctor, my headache is gone."

He says, "The doctor is out. I'm just another patient."

You say (shrewdly): "Then, I take it, there will be no fee."

Thrift is a virtue men like to find in a woman.   MISS H. P.

13

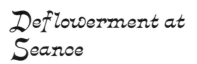

Deflowerment at Seance

At seance conducted by smooth-talking gypsy, you ask him to produce spirit of Rudolph Valentino. Spirit of Valentino appears and you are deflowered.

After deflowerment, you say, "Gee, Mr. Valentino, may I have your autograph?"

He says, "To tell the truth, this whole seance is a fake."

You say: "Personally, I don't believe in them either."

Gypsies, when accepted as equals, can be relied upon to tell the truth. MISS H. P.

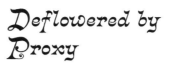

Deflowered by Proxy

You fall in love with pen pal, Walter, English turf accountant, whom you have never met. By correspondence, wedding date is set. Two days before marriage, he cables that he can't leave London due to pressing business deal. Instead, according to cable, he has made arrangements for proxy marriage and his friend, Howard, on 84th Street, will stand up for him. You invite Howard to your apartment following ceremony. After deflowerment, you say, "Incidentally, Howard..." He says, "There is no Howard. I'm Walter, your pen pal."

You say: "Of course, silly, I recognized your handwriting on the marriage certificate."

When married to practical joker, it is always delightfully feminine to go along with gag. MISS H. P.

Deflowered by Chinese Detective

You are one of twelve weekend guests at Lord Pilroy's old castle on Scottish moors when Lord Pilroy is done in by murderer. That night, Chinese detective arrives at castle and questions everyone in private.

Your alibi is that you last saw Lord Pilroy leaving through your bedroom window after he stealthily deflowered you in your sleep.

Chinese detective asks you to re-enact that scene.

Then he says, "Long finger of accusation points to you as murderer. Lord Pilroy obviously did not deflower you—because *I* have flower."

You say: "You're not as smart as you think, Chan. You destroyed the evidence yourself."

Moreover, no court in the land would accept such flimsy evidence.

MISS H. P.

Deflowered and Thrust Aside (Like an Old Glove)

Two weeks have passed since losing of flower to Method actor and he has made absolutely no attempt to see you. You are walking along street in sunshine on bright afternoon, wondering, wondering, wondering. Suddenly he appears walking in opposite direction. You recognize him by his dungarees. You smile encouragingly and say, "I hear you've been away at summer stock." He says, "In the middle of winter?"

You say (frivolously): "The theatre is such mad make-believe."

Through the magic of the theatre you can express yourself fully in every season. MISS H. P.

21

Deflowered by Famous Crooner

Famous crooner visits town on one night stand, and through a series of lucky breaks, you get autograph. After deflowerment, he leaves town and when you tell story to girl friends, they do not believe you. You refuse to be laughing stock. On crooner's return engagement at local theatre, you storm his dressing room with mob of skeptical girl friends. You show autograph to crooner to refresh his memory. He says, "That's not my handwriting."

You say: "Then may I come back for your real autograph later?"

Obviously, someone in this situation is completely confused.

MISS H. P.

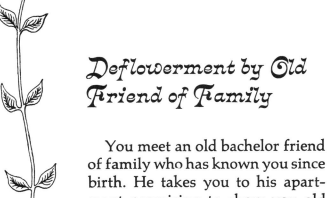

Deflowerment by Old Friend of Family

You meet an old bachelor friend of family who has known you since birth. He takes you to his apartment promising to show you old tintypes of your parents. After deflowerment, you ask to see pictures. He says, "There are no pictures, but your parents are in the next room."

You say: "Golly, I love surprises."

One of your relatives is sure to have a family album. MISS H. P.

Deflowered by Perfect Stranger

You are approached on street by perfect stranger. After deflowerment, you say, "Gee, I never thought it would happen this way, with a perfect stranger." He says, "You mean you are not Marge my fiancee? You look exactly like her. I have made a terrible mistake, Miss."

You say (inventively): "Why, I completely forgot! I *am* Marge, your fiancee."

This young man sounds like a complete dunderhead to me. It is quite likely that you can sustain your little masquerade with this dolt and actually bring him to the altar, without him ever realizing it was a case of mistaken identity.

MISS H. P.

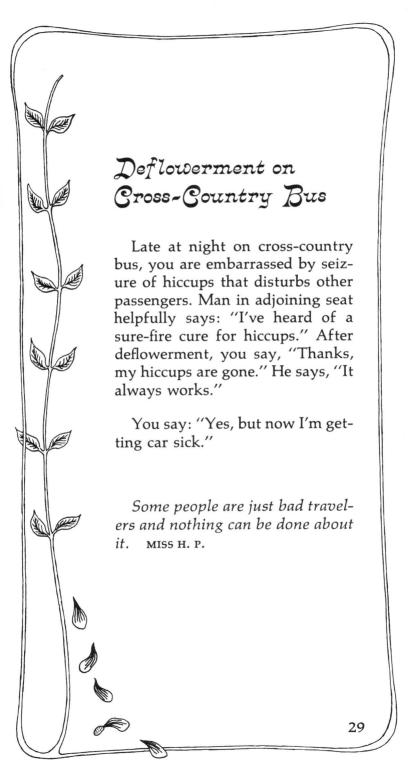

Deflowerment on Cross-Country Bus

Late at night on cross-country bus, you are embarrassed by seizure of hiccups that disturbs other passengers. Man in adjoining seat helpfully says: "I've heard of a sure-fire cure for hiccups." After deflowerment, you say, "Thanks, my hiccups are gone." He says, "It always works."

You say: "Yes, but now I'm getting car sick."

Some people are just bad travelers and nothing can be done about it. MISS H. P.

Deflowerment on American Express Tour

You are on American Express tour of Paris night life. Bus unloads at Café Aux Apaches, a low dive in Latin Quarter. No sooner do you enter dark, smoke-filled cabaret than you find yourself whisked into Apache dance, which ends with your being deflowered in full view of applauding patrons. As handsome Apache dancer escorts you back to table with other tourists, he whispers into your ear, "Not bad, I can probably get you a three-week engagement here."

You say: "Merci, Non."

Pay in Parisian night clubs is notoriously low.   MISS H. P.

Deflowerment While Baby Sitting

Having advertised your baby sitting services in the local newspaper, you receive phone call from gentleman who gives you his address. On arrival, you meet young man of college age. You ask "Where's the baby?" He says, "I'm the baby." After deflowerment, you say, "What time are your parents coming home?" He says, "Sadly enough, I'm an orphan."

You say: "No wonder you wanted a baby sitter."

As a baby sitter, you must always insist that you meet the child's parents. MISS H. P.

Deflowered by Elevator Operator

Deflowerment takes place on elevator stuck between floors for three hours. Later, back in penthouse apartment, you realize social difficulties involved in future rides with elevator man. Next morning, off to luncheon of Junior League, you summon elevator. Door opens and he says, as always, "Down, Miss?"

You say (staring directly ahead): "Yes as quickly as possible please."

The best thing to do under the circumstances is to pretend you are completely engrossed in the ride—whether Up or Down. MISS H. P.

35

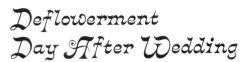

Deflowerment Day After Wedding

On first night of marriage, husband fails to gather flower. Next morning, you ask him to get you bromo seltzer. Miserably unhappy, he leaves hotel room and after three hours, still has not returned. You ring room service and order bromo seltzer. Handsome bell boy appears and after deflowerment, you say to bell boy, "Where is my bromo seltzer?" He says, "We're out of bromo seltzer." At that moment, husband knocks on door and says, "I had to walk all over town to find bromo seltzer."

You say (vexed): "Tell the bell-boy where you got it!"

You are entirely justified in being vexed in such a situation. It would be perfectly natural for a girl to expect the hotel to have some bromo seltzer. MISS H. P.

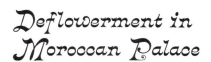

Deflowerment in Moroccan Palace

On Cook's tour of Moroccan palace, you get lost in corridor and ask eunuch where rest of tour has gone. Smiling eunuch ushers you through ornate door and you find yourself inside lavish harem where you are promptly deflowered by Sultan. After deflowerment, he says, "You are not one of my regular wives. Chop off the imposter's head."

You say: "Gee, I saw a movie like this once, starring Turhan Bey."

A last-minute attempt at flattery which just might work. MISS H. P.

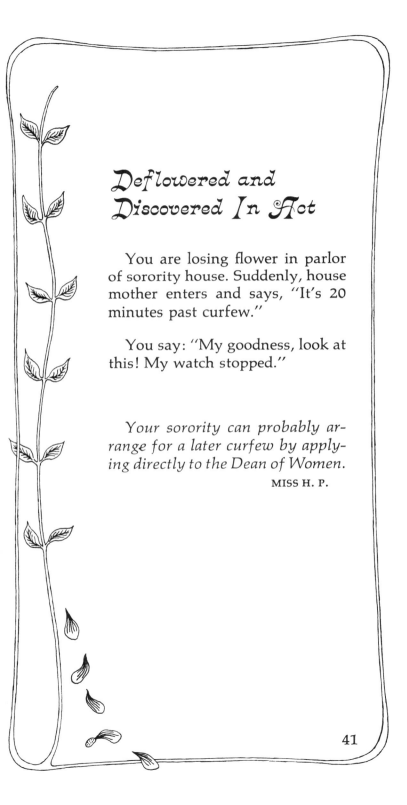

Deflowered and Discovered In Act

You are losing flower in parlor of sorority house. Suddenly, house mother enters and says, "It's 20 minutes past curfew."

You say: "My goodness, look at this! My watch stopped."

Your sorority can probably arrange for a later curfew by applying directly to the Dean of Women.

MISS H. P.

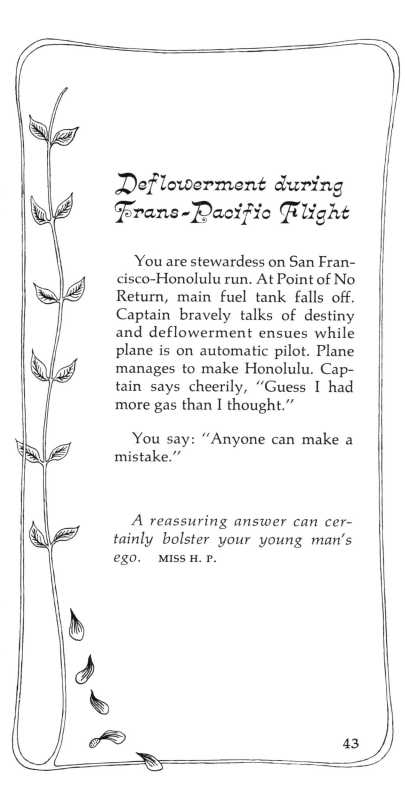

Deflowerment during Trans-Pacific Flight

You are stewardess on San Francisco-Honolulu run. At Point of No Return, main fuel tank falls off. Captain bravely talks of destiny and deflowerment ensues while plane is on automatic pilot. Plane manages to make Honolulu. Captain says cheerily, "Guess I had more gas than I thought."

You say: "Anyone can make a mistake."

A reassuring answer can certainly bolster your young man's ego. MISS H. P.

Deflowerment in Chinatown

On sightseeing tour of China-town you stop at small gift shop. As guide and rest of tourists leave shop, mysterious Oriental beckons you into back room promising you special price on backscratchers you want to send to folks at home. He offers you lichee nuts. As you pass out the thought occurs to you that they are drugged. After deflower-ment you say: "I still feel dizzy from those drugged lichees." Mys-terious Oriental says, "They're or-dinary lichee nuts, Miss."

You say: "Come to think of it, even ordinary lichee nuts make me dizzy."

All lichee nuts should be avoided anyway as they are bad for the teeth. MISS H. P.

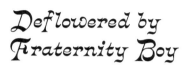

Deflowered by Fraternity Boy

You lose flower to Roger but win his fraternity pin. Next day you encounter campus queen. You notice she is wearing identical pin. "Oh," you say warmly, "I see you are also pinned to a Gamma Gamma Gamma. Which one?" Campus queen smiles, "Why to Roger, of course."

You say, lovingly: "Roger is awfully generous."

A smart girl will always find opportunities to compliment her young man in the presence of others. MISS H. P.

A NOTE ON THE AUTHORS

Edward St. John Gorey (1925–2000) gave to the world over one hundred works, including *The Gashlycrumb Tinies*, *The Doubtful Guest*, *The Haunted Tea-cosy*, *The Glorious Nosebleed*, *The Curious Sofa*, *The Epiplectic Bicycle*, *The Headless Bust*, *The Iron Tonic*, *The Other Statue*, *The Unstrung Harp*, *The Willowdale Handcar* and *The West Wing* (all available from Bloomsbury); prizewinning set and costume designs for innumerable theater productions from Cape Cod to Broadway; a remarkable number of illustrations in publications such as the *New Yorker* and the *New York Times*; and the instantly recognizable animations for PBS's *Mystery!* series. Gorey's masterful pen-and-ink illustrations and his ironic, offbeat humor have brought him critical acclaim and an avid following throughout the world.

Mel Juffe (1929–2005), a writer, editor, reporter, political analyst, and teacher, worked at Radio Free Europe, the *New York Journal American*, *Eye* magazine, the Foreign Policy Association, New York University, and the *New York Post*. He is the author of the novel *Flash*.